An Eton
Schoolboy's
Album

This book is dedicated to my parents, who *put me down*★
for Eton before I was born. (They also *put me down* for
a girl's school just in case.)

★Often a place is reserved for you at Eton. It is not unusual for this
to take place before your birth.

An Eton Schoolboy's Album

Mark Dixon

DEBRETT'S PEERAGE LIMITED

ISBN 0 905649 78 8

Copyright © Mark Dixon, 1985

First published in 1985 by Debrett's Peerage Limited,
73-77 Britannia Road, London SW6 2JR
represented by Webb & Bower (Publishers) Ltd,
9 Colleton Crescent, Exeter, Devon, EX2 4BY
distributed by J.M. Dent & Sons (Sales) Ltd,
Dunhams Lane, Letchworth, Herts, SG6 1LF

Designed by Andrew Ivett
Typeset in Bembo by Oxford Computer Typesetting
Printed and bound in Great Britain by R.J. Acford, Chichester

Foreword

Fifty years ago it would, I suspect, have been customary for anyone writing a foreword to a book of this kind to say that his days at Eton had been the happiest of his life; and I myself can remember at least half a dozen elderly gentlemen, a generation or two older than I, who looked back on their old school with an almost obsessive affection — to the point where one formed the impression that the whole of their subsequent existence had been one long anti-climax. But times have changed; and I doubt whether any readers of this book will be in the slightest degree shocked or even surprised if I now record that although my own Eton days were quite happy enough, I have been — almost consistently — a good deal happier since.

This was not, heaven knows, Eton's fault. Every school has to exert discipline and restrict individual liberty, and such measures are never popular among those at the receiving end. Admittedly, vast numbers of the rules and regulations from which we suffered have since been swept away, and quite right too; but I do not in the least blame Eton for imposing them in the first place; they were merely reflections of a sterner, severer age — an age, incidentally, in which most other public schools were positive penitentiaries in comparison. Anyway, there were — as one worked one's way up the school — immense compensations. Athletic prowess brought rewards in glory and prestige that a Coe or a McEnroe might envy; academic brilliance might earn one a place in Sixth Form Select and the many priviliges that came with it. The really successful Etonian in his last year — Captain of his house, and perhaps of the Boats as well, President of Pop and a member of Sixth Form Select — possessed, in his own little Eton microcosm, a degree of power and authority such as is given to few of us at any time in our lives. To such a Superman, when the time came for him to live in the outside world, the harsh realities of the daily grind must have come as a nasty jolt indeed.

The only trouble was that there were a large number of boys, like myself, who excelled in neither field — who never made Sixth Form Select and who wore a scug cap throughout their Eton days. Even then, I doubt whether most of us really minded; but we did, as I remember, frequently observe to each other how pleasant it would be to have someone to run errands for us instead of constantly running them for other people, to clean our shoes, cook our teas, and — most important of all — lay our fires.

The cold — that is what I remember most: the cold of those wartime winters. There was no central heating, and though we each had a room of our own we were allowed a fire, in the tiniest fireplace imaginable, only every *other* night. Hot baths were rationed too — to five inches of water, twice a week. Food, what there was of it, offered little comfort; try as I may to prevent it, my mind still occasionally harks back to those February mornings when one awoke, frozen to the marrow, at seven, stayed in bed — battling with the cold — till 7.25, dressed in a flash (no question of washing) and then sped out into the icy dark to be at Early School, perhaps several hundred yards away, by 7.30. Fifty minutes later one returned, ravenous, to a breakfast consisting of a slice of spam or a warm blancmange of powdered egg. Only a few weeks before his death, the late Lord Harlech confirmed to me the truth of a story I had often heard: the story of how, during his time at Eton, one of his schoolfellows had committed suicide. The next evening his housemaster summoned a shocked house together after prayers, and asked if anyone could suggest a reason that might have led to this tragic occurrence. The infant Harlech (or Ormsby-Gore as he was then) slowly raised his hand. "Could it have been the food, Sir?" he asked.

So much for the debits; but these, even for the undistinguished like me, were easily outweighed by the credits. First, I think, was the sheer strength of the school's own personality. It was like living at close quarters with a hugely intelligent uncle: occasionally cantankerous, often illogical, but invariably stimulating and ultimately benevolent. You might feel irritated, frustrated, hard done by, you might even at moments long to wring his neck; but he made you think, he made you laugh, he took endless trouble over you, and he never ceased to take a tremendous interest in everything you said and did. Never, absolutely never, were you bored. And you always knew, in your heart, how prodigiously lucky you were to have him around.

Secondly, there was the beauty that encompassed you. Now teenage boys are not normally noted for a high degree of aesthetic appreciation, and I suspect that most of us took our surroundings very much for granted. Subconsciously, however, we soaked them up — the marvellously mellow brick of School Yard, the wall-paintings in the Chapel, the broad acres of Sixpenny and Agar's Plough, the cool, gentle sweep of the Thames round Fellows' Eyot. There was, too, a feeling of spaciousness that exists, so far as I am aware, at few other schools. We had friends by the dozen if we needed them; at the same time, when the need arose, it was never difficult to be alone.

Temperamentally, I have never been one of Nature's Old Boys. Not once in my life have I ever donned an Old Etonian tie and, except when parental duty has made it impossible, I have avoided the Fourth of June like the Plague. This not through any lack of affection for Eton, nor of gratitude for all it gave me; it is simply because I have an inborn fear of nostalgia and would rather look forward to things than look back on them. It does mean, on the other hand, that there are countless facets of Eton life which I had — or thought I had — completely forgotten; and I am astonished by the number of these that Mark Dixon's splendid photographs, by some almost Proustian alchemy, have brought flooding back into my mind. I am all the more delighted to have the opportunity of commending this book to all those anxious to capture — or, in the case of my old school-fellows, to recapture — something of that odd, quirkish, elusive magic of a school which, for better or for worse, has made so many of us what we are today.

John Julius Norwich

Acknowledgements

my family

Adam Blaker, O.E., my cousin
Hugo Dixon, O.E., K.S., my brother
Piers Dixon, O.E., K.S., my father
Lord Duncan-Sandys, O.E., my grandfather
Julian Sandys, O.E., my uncle

my contemporaries

Jonathan Butcher, O.E.
Alexander Cohane, O.E.
Jonathan Chattey, O.E.
Darius Guppy, O.E.
Charles Harman, O.E.
Paddy Meade, O.E.
Matthew Fraser Moat, O.E.
Nicholas Rowley, O.E.

and

Miss Andrews, my *boy's maid*
Tony Butler, my *modern tutor*
Mrs. Ellam, my *dame*
Dick Haddon, my second *housemaster*
"Hatty" Jaques, my Latin *beak*
Michael Kidson, my history *beak*
Michael McCrum, the *head master*
Pete Needham, my *classical tutor*
The Reverend Roger Royle, the *conduct*
Ken Spencer, my first *housemaster*

and

Robert Ducas, O.E., my literary agent
Martin Stansfeld, O.E., my editor

and to the following who do not come with the above illustrious affixes

Beth Boatright, Veronica Boswell, Francesca Brydon, Diana Burlton, David Cantor, Fionna Cardale, Charles Churchill, Bryan Colmer, Louise Duncan, Roddy Fisher, Caroline Franks, William Grant, Antony Haden-Guest, Claire Harrison, Leo Heaps, Norman Hickman, Craig Jenks, Tina Jorgensen, Peter Lawrence, Guy Lesser, Nigel Linacre, Sue Linacre, Ann Mavroleon, Bill McDougall, Pamela Milne, Gerard Mizrahi, Melanie Parker, Ping Ping Qiu, Edwina Sandys, Laura Sandys, James Snedeker, John Train, Charlotte Rutherford, Tarik Wildman

O.E. = Old Etonian.

K.S. = King's Scholar.

boy's maid = The maid who assists about fifteen Etonians with their cleaning.

modern tutor = The master who succeeds your *classical tutor* and who looks after your academic life once you are sixteen. You select him yourself.

dame = The matron in charge of a *house*. It is a prime job for a spinster who wishes to have a lot of children. You must refer to her as "Ma'am".

housemaster = The master in charge of each *house*.

beak = Master.

head master = Eton's headmaster is spelt as two words. He is usually referred to as *head man* by the boys.

classical tutor = The master who is responsible for your academic life until you are sixteen.

conduct = Eton's senior chaplain.

house = A group of about fifty boys who live in the same house.

Photo by Hugo Dixon

Author's note

I spent most of my five years at Eton taking photographs. The rest of my time I was avoiding the *field game* and explaining why my academic work wasn't done on time. While many Etonians tried to win sports cups and academic prizes, my only serious achievement was winning the *Peter Fleming Owl*. As a photographer, I'm embarrassed to admit that the only other award I received was for the *Chronicle's* "Most Irrelevant Photograph".

Occasionally, I would take time off from my photography to scramble through a *Latin construe* or history essay. My road was not one that led me to great academic heights. Nor did I leave Eton able to play the *wall game* or *fives*. But I did find myself, at the end of my Eton career, with a portfolio of eight thousand photographs: pictures of Etonians, *beaks*, *dames*, *boys maids*, the *field game*, the *wall game* and rowing; photos of boys in *div*, in *Rowlands*, in *Tap* and playing in the snow. In short, the upstairs and downstairs of Eton.

field game = Eton's home-grown combination of soccer and rugby football, played with a round ball.

Peter Fleming Owl = A bronze owl, awarded for the best contribution to the *Chronicle* each *half*. In memory of Peter Fleming O.E., writer, sportsman and Ian's brother.

Chronicle = The school's fortnightly magazine.

Latin construe = Translation from a Latin text such as Caesar's 'Gallic Wars'. In a *construe test* any boy can be called upon to translate out loud.

wall game = A ball game unique to Eton, which is played against the *Wall*.

fives = Like squash, but played with the hands instead of a racket. It originates from the time when boys played a home-made ball game against one of the buttresses of *College Chapel*. Part of the buttress is reproduced in the modern *fives* court, which can be found as far away as Nigeria. There are two theories of how *fives* got its name. The nineteenth-century slang for "hand" was "fives" as in "I must wash my fives". Also the game may originally have been played between two teams, each of five players.

div = Abbreviation for *division*, meaning a lesson.

Rowlands = The tuck shop.

Tap = The school's pub.

My brother

Dear Mr. Dixon,

Mark got through Common Entrance with flying colours, as you will have heard.

Raef Payne, alas, has no room for him, but I have made successful overtures to Norman Addison, who will be delighted to take Mark in January. May I suggest you get in touch with him straight away. He is:

C.N.C.Addison,
Farrer House,
Eton College,
Windsor. SL4 6EE.

Telephone No. Windsor 65613.

Yours sincerely,

David Macindoe

P. Dixon Esq.,
22, Ponsonby Terrace,
LONDON SW1P 4QA.

I first visited Eton four months before I was born.

My parents were keen to secure the best *housemaster*. To come up with their first choice, my father had taken a survey of all the Etonians he knew. They had all ranked their own *housemaster* first, of course, but Mr. Payne had come out a steady second. So my parents went to see him and reserve me a place in his *house*. He was more than delighted. After all, not all parents book so early.

Thirteen years later I got good news and bad news. The good news was that I had passed *Common Entrance* and would be going to Eton in September. The bad news was that Mr. Payne had overbooked. Someone would have to be dropped and he had chosen me. I didn't know why, but as I hadn't chosen him I didn't much mind.

It was with some disappointment though, at this last minute change, that my parents drove Nanny and me down to Eton to meet the replacement *housemaster*.

Mr. Spencer was standing in the hall with his *dame*, Mrs Ellam, and his wife, Anne, who had been a *dame* before. My mother was telling the *housemaster's* wife how beautiful the garden was (who was quick to point out that it was strictly out-of-bounds to the boys — Mrs. Spencer didn't want her roses trampled on).

Nanny was in serious conversation with the *dame*. They were running down the *clothes list*. My father and Mr. Spencer were talking about Latin and Greek.

They were all immersed in a long and enthusiastic conversation.

"You are so clever to get roses to bloom so late in the season."
"About Latin, will you teach him the modern pronunciation?"
"Do all his socks have to be black?"
"Or will he use the Classical?"
"Can I pack some extra grey ones for him?"
"But when I was at Eton everybody learnt Ancient Greek."
"Should the name tapes be done in Old English script?"
"I know it's not compulsory, but we would like him to take Greek all the same."
"How many pairs of garters did you say?"

I was a little boy in a deep armchair and I sank even deeper.
"Latin socks?... Greek name tapes?..."

The conversation continued.
I knew I was at Eton.

Common Entrance = The standard exam adopted by all public schools.

clothes list = The very long list of clothes, which every *new boy* has to arrive with. It includes twelve handkerchiefs and two tailcoats.

The Eton Coat of Arms

On your first day at Eton you are bombarded with information, appointments and obligations. There are new faces that will be offended if they are not remembered. New places to find your way to and no map. A different language and no dictionary. And at the end of your first three weeks you are given a *colours' test*.

The Eton language has about three hundred words: nouns, adjectives, and verbs. You're not only expected to understand it from day one, but speak it as well. Let "master" slip instead of *beak*, or "lesson" instead of *div*, and you'll see faces around you fall. I never learnt as many as three hundred words of Latin or French at my private school. Within a few days at Eton I had another language under my belt.

Your first week at Eton is a rat race. It must be one of the toughest tests you'll ever have to take. You can't practise before you arrive. On your first day you'll encounter collars and studs you thought went out with the last century. The first morning it's all much harder; the stud won't go through the collar because it's starched stiff and not yet broken in. And if you do manage to get the stud through, where do you put the little white tie with a hole in it? Under or over the collar? I went for help to the room next door: my neighbour had the same problem. He was a *new boy* too.

You don't have time to sit down and realize the pickle you're in. There are *divs* to go to on the first day. You think the *beak* is going to test you on your Latin and French *irregulars*. You know you had them somewhere handy when you took *Common Entrance,* but where have they gone now? Try chasing an irregular verb down memory lane when you're late for your first *div* and you've got the wrong books and you're not sure you're in the right *div* anyway. Try remembering the scan of a *hexameter* or *pentameter* when you're jittering at a quite different rhythm yourself.

colours' test = A test given to *new boys* after three weeks at Eton. It covers the school and *house* colours; the Eton language, history and geography.
new boy = An Etonian in his first *half.*
irregulars = Irregular verbs, either Latin or French.
hexameter = A line of Latin verse with six metres.
pentameter = A line of Latin verse with five metres.

When you've got through the morning you soon realize that the *field game*, as unique as it might be, is a long way from extinction. I watched it more than I played it. Either I was photographing for the *Chronicle* or I was armed with some other *slack bob* excuse. I never learnt its rules or understood its language.

There are an unlimited number of fouls and, when you commit one of these, you will hear the eleven voices of your opponents ring out in protest to the umpire:

"*Cornering*, that man!"
"He's *furking*!"
"That man's *passing*!"
"He's *sneaking*!"
"I saw him *move before*!"
"He was *playing on the ground*!"
"No, he was *kneeling on the ball*!"

Although there is a select group that does understand the rules, this does not necessarily include the players. Because the umpire himself is often in the dark, the players are encouraged to appeal. Half the game is spent in argument.

If you want to win you may begin by scoring a *rouge* by touching the ball down behind the line. Then your aim is to convert the *rouge* to a *goal*. To make this conversion a *ram* is used. The human battering ram consists of three of the heaviest boys holding onto each other's waists. Jumping up and down in time to the words, they shout at the top of their voices: "Left up, right up, left up, right up. One, two, three, RAM!". Then with their heads down they rush forward into the *post's* stomach, hoping to release the ball that is held in between his feet. If they succeed they score what is called a *rammed rouge*. The *post* is stopped from fleeing by the two *side posts*, whose sole job it is to hold him in place.

slack bob = Technically, a boy in the Summer *half* who is neither a *wet bob* nor a *dry bob*. It can also be used to describe someone who avoids playing sports at any time of the year.

cornering	
furking	
passing	Field game fouls
sneaking	of one sort or another
move before	
playing on the ground	
kneeling on the ball	

rouge = A touchdown worth two points.

goal = A score worth three points.

ram = A human battering ram used to convert a *rouge* to a *goal*.

post = The least coveted position in the *field game*.

rammed rouge = A goal scored by successfully *ramming* a *rouge*.

side post = The two players who support the *post*.

Oranges at half-time

An appeal

I didn't learn much history at Eton★, but one of the first things we were taught was that Henry VI founded Eton, his "College Roiall of oure Lady Eton", in the year 1440. He was only nineteen. His statue, which stands in School Yard, is important to all Etonians but particularly to the *tugs* — the *King's Scholars*. It was for them that he founded the school. In his royal charter he decreed that seventy "poore scollers" should be educated.

His statue was put up in 1719 and by 1938 it had accumulated a marvellous green patina. The *head man* wanted it cleaned. As a sample of what he intended a small part of the Founder's right leg was polished. Boys, *beaks, dames* and *O.E.s* were in uproar and so the project was scrapped. In the late Seventies things were not so democratic. This time the *provost* made his move while Eton was asleep, and Eton woke up to find a shiny founder.

★ My history *beak*, Michael Kidson, reported to my parents once: "I very much wish I could be cheerful about Dixon's O level prospects — but I can't. He is a terribly bad historian".

tug = The Etonian's name for the scholar of Eton. Also called *King's Scholar* and *colleger*. Some think that the word *tug* derives from the Latin *togati*, meaning "gowned". Others say that the *tugs* got their name because the *oppidans* were always tugging at their gowns.

King's Scholar = *Tug*.

head man = The *head master*.

provost = Elected by the *fellows*, he is chairman of Eton's governing body.

The Founder's statue

Right: the Founder
reflected in a puddle

Fagging is one of Eton's oldest, most famous and most criticized traditions. Etonians in their first year are obliged to act as servants to Etonians in their last year and each morning the *fag* must report to his *fag master* to clean his shoes, make his bed and run errands.

After lunch there is usually a *boy call*. A member of *library* bellows down the stairs "Boooooooooo Yee UP!". The phrase lasts five seconds and echoes through the corridors long after. If you are a *fag* you respond immediately by scrambling towards the *library* at top speed. It doesn't matter what you were doing before the call, your only interest is to reach the *library* as quickly as possible. It is entirely acceptable to elbow your friends out of the way. You jump into the queue and if you're the unlucky last one you get the errand. You might have to run messages back and forth between two *houses* arranging a cricket match. Or you may be sent on a run to Windsor to find out what's on at the cinema.

Etonians don't use the telephone and it may be one of the only places left where much of the communication is still done by runners. Though the school felt sorry for the *fags* and installed an inter-house telephone, this worked badly. It had only one line on which conversations from all twenty-six *houses* were attempted simultaneously.

My nanny was also my uncle's nanny, and, as he had been at Eton, I knew all about *fagging* before I arrived. You can imagine my relief when I discovered that I was in one of the few houses which had abolished it. Our *house* did have a similar institution called *library table* which involved washing the *library's* dishes as punishment for certain petty crimes. A friend of mine was put on *library table* for a reason he thought unfair. His appeals fell on deaf ears until the clatter of breaking dishes drew a distraught *library* member to the kitchen. "They just slipped out of my hands", he explained.

library = 1. The self-elective governing body of each *house* made up of Etonians in their last year.
2. The room belonging to members of *library* where they have a television set and refrigerator, but not many books.

Etonians playing Etonian *fags* in a *house* play

When Henry VI founded Eton he intended the chapel to be twice its present size. A little plaque half-way down Keate's Lane marks its planned length. When Henry died Eton ran out of money and could only afford a wooden roof. There was no question of completing the whole structure.

But after the Second World War Eton ran into some money and began building new *houses*, swimming pools, a theatre and Bekynton (originally called the 'Central Feeding Complex'). A group of Etonians who knew their Eton history wrote a letter to the *Chronicle*. They maintained that it would have been the Founder's wish for the money to be spent on knocking down the buildings around Keate's Lane, diverting the High Street, and extending *College Chapel* to the length Henry intended. But the idea was never taken seriously.

In his royal charter Henry had instructed the school to pray for his soul once a week for eternity. Today, more than five hundred years later, the *tugs* still do — in medieval Latin.

Each morning at 8.50, ten minutes before Chapel, the bell starts to ring. After five minutes it stops and every Etonian in every corner of Eton knowns he has precisely five minutes to be in his pew. In this vast game of musical chairs, involving some 1200 boys and three different chapel destinations★, you lose if you are not in your seat before the bell tolls five more times.

The Reverend Roger Royle, who was *conduct* for most of my time, left Eton to become Britain's show business vicar. Eton's only non-Oxbridge *conduct*, Mr. Royle is best remembered for making religion fun. In one sermon he told us that supermarkets are dangerous places because women steer the trollies.

Eton has its Chapel problems. Boys often put their waistcoat buttons into the collection bag if they run out of change. *Sermon cricket*, a sport you won't find listed in the *fixtures*, is still occasionally played, and is as popular with the *wet bobs* as *dry bobs*. A similar sport was the rage in our parents' generation at the time when Alington was *head man*. Famous for the hymns he wrote for Eton's own hymn book, he was even more famous for the length of his sermons. Bets were taken on the number of times, in order to fill a gap, he would say, "Grass is not always green". My *conduct* had to deal with one fad after another. First he had to tackle *kneeler football* and later the slamming of hymn books.

In the run up to *trials*, there are two types of Etonians with very different exam-passing techniques. Royle told me once: "Some become very religious and can be seen in deep prayer. Others *appear* to be in prayer, kneeling with their heads very low, but on closer inspection it is clear they are not. They have their *trials* notes handy and are *swotting* instead."

★ The three chapel destinations are *College Chapel, Lower Chapel*, and *D-Worship*.

Bekynton = The central feeding complex where about ten houses are fed. It is named after Bishop Bekynton, Henry VI's secretary.

College Chapel = Eton's main chapel erected by Henry VI in 1441. He laid the foundation stone on Passion Sunday.

Sermon cricket = More of a gambling game than a cricket game, based on the number of "Ummms" and "Ahhhs" in a sermon.

fixtures = A pocket-sized compendium carried by almost every Etonian, which includes the *half's* sports events.

wet bob = A rower.

dry bob = A cricketer.

kneeler football = The chapel kneelers are used instead of a ball. The rules are closer to those of the *wall game* than the *field game*, the pew representing the *Wall*.

trials = School exams at the end of most *halves*.

swotting = Studying intensively.

A Passion Play

While most preachers were boring, others went out of their way to entertain or even to shock. One who visited *Lower Chapel* was illustrating the idea of Belief. He began with the words: "What would your friends in *College Chapel* say if you told them I started my sermon by peeling a banana and eating it?" And then he promptly did just that. Another visiting parson began with an even more extraordinary opening stunt. "Wherefore if thy hand or thy foot offend thee, cut them off, and cast them from thee", he declared. We had heard that passage many times before but this time things were different: the preacher unscrewed his false arm and hurled it into the air. A few boys sitting on the *knife boards* nearly fell off.

But the boys had their fun as well. One *C-Sunday* a huge group of boys turned up to the Holy Communion service. The vergers, led by the *holy poker*, counted their number and an extra large amount of wine was duly consecrated. But, as planned, only a small handful of boys took Communion. The abstainers watched the chaplains with amusement. There was a large amount of consecrated wine left over, and, as anyone who has been confirmed knows, once consecrated it has to be drunk.

Most boys are confirmed while they are still at Eton, but not simply for spiritual reasons. One friend explained to me that, because of a loop-hole in the *marking out* system, if you are confirmed you can skip chapel on a *C-Sunday* without being detected. But the most amusing reason came from a friend's mother: "It is so embarrassing for us at Easter because he can't take Communion in the parish".

Every *new boy* is auditioned for the *College Chapel* choir and successful candidates always regret the consequences. So on my brother's first day at Eton I gave him two words of advice: "Sing badly". He did sing badly and was pleased when the *College Chapel* choir rejected him. But instead he found himself in the *Lower Chapel* choir, which is considered even worse.

Lower Chapel = The chapel used by Etonians in *E* and *F-blocks*. The area in *Lower Chapel* reserved for *new boys* is called the *Hencoop*.

knife boards = The rows of pews on each side of the aisle in *College Chapel*, which are barely wide enough to sit on.

C-Sunday = A Sunday morning service in *College Chapel* where Holy Communion is celebrated.

holy poker = *College Chapel's* verger, who leads guests with his verge (wand) held high above his head.

marking out = The system by which Etonians who shirk Chapel are usually caught.

In the Michaelmas and Lent *halves, lock up* is at
6.15pm. In the Summer *half* it is at 7.45pm. After
lock-up you are not expected to relax. There are *E.W.s*
to do. These were the hours when I had to grapple
with *Latin construe:* a translation from Latin into
English. There are two ways to prepare yourself for
the following day's *construe test.* Either you make sure
you understand the whole text and will be able to
translate it word for word. Or you buy a translation
from Alden & Blackwell's on the High Street and
memorize it. The latter is the more dangerous because
the *beak* might ask you to explain how you arrived at
your answer. Nor does this route teach you much
Latin.

half = Term. The word originates from the days when the school
year was divided into two halves. To describe half-term, Etonians
have resisted the temptation to coin the word 'half-half'. Instead
they call it *long leave.*
lock-up = The time when you have to be inside your *house.* The
doors are actually locked.

E.W. = Abbreviation for *extra work*, or homework.
construe test = In a *construe test* any boy can be called upon to
translate from Latin out loud.

My memories of Latin are a jumble. Ablative absolutes. Adverbial accusatives. Gerunds, gerundives and supines. Conjunctions, co-ordinative and subordinative.

Conjugations of verbs. Declensions of nouns. The nominative, vocative and accusative cases. The irregular, impersonal and defective verbs. The masculine, feminine and neuter nouns. And a *div* reciting, "Hic, haec, hoc... Hunc, hanc, hoc... Huius, huius, huius... Huic, huic, huic... Hōc, hāc, hōc." Mixed moments of mythology. Virgil's *Iliad* with the Greeks inside the burning city. Was it Troy? King Priam meeting his murderer and calling him a "degenerate", a word I didn't know in English, let alone in Latin. But I continued *construing* as far as the Death of Dido.

After you've had supper you've got half an hour before *absence* is read. This roll call is taken to establish that no one has escaped to Windsor to drink. For years boys have wondered why *absence* wasn't called presence.

absence = A roll call taken by *housemasters* at 8.30 each evening. In the Summer *half* there is also a 5.30pm absence.

After *lights out* at 10pm your *housemaster*, members of *library* and members of *debate* pace the corridors in search of light escaping under the door or through the key hole. Some boys wire their lights so that as soon as the door is opened the lights automatically switch off. One officious member of *debate* caught me with my lights on a few minutes after ten. The argument that ensued resulted in my having to write two hundred lines: "I must not say shut up to Debate".

lights out = The time when you have to be in bed with your lights out. In your first *half*, *lights out* is at 9.00pm. After that, it is at 9.30pm until you are in *C-block* when it is at 10.00pm.

debate = The governing body of each *house*, and elected by the *library*. It consists mainly of boys in *C-block*.

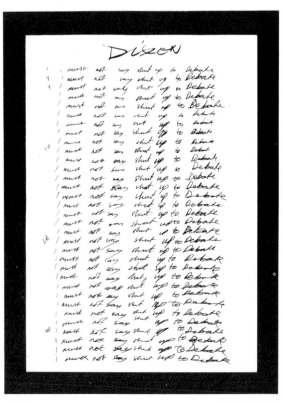

My room

If your *beak* considers you have gone beyond the call of duty on a piece of work, he might give you a *sent up for good*. The work is then copied onto a specially printed form and shown to the *head man*. In my five years at Eton I was not once *sent up for good*.

Or, if he thinks you have pulled your socks up, he might give you a *commended for good effort*. One of my only *commended for good efforts* was not the blessing it seemed. After months at the bottom of my geography *div* one week I did slightly better, for no reason apparent to me. The *beak*, convinced that I had finally turned over a new leaf, generously gave me a *commended*. Both my *housemaster* and the *head man* were over the moon until my attempts at explaining this

progress proved entirely unconvincing. It did me more bad than good.

Your *beak* can also give out *show ups* and *rips*. A *show up* is for good work and you can show it to your *housemaster* and *classical tutor*. A *rip* is bad and you have to show it to both. It is a most demoralizing experience to receive one. The *beak*, often in a rage to justify his action, rips your work in front of the *division*. Whenever I got a *show up* (and that was very rare) I would hold on to it in anticipation of a flood of *rips* that were due the following week. When the *rips* arrived, I presented them to my *tutors* with the *show up* sticking out of the bunch, hoping that this would persuade them I was not *all* bad.

division = A class of boys.

COMMENDED FOR GOOD EFFORT

Name *Dixa mi*

Block *D* *Michaelmas* Half 1977

SUBJECT: DIVISION MASTER:

Geography *JtV*

Classical/Modern Tutor: House Master:

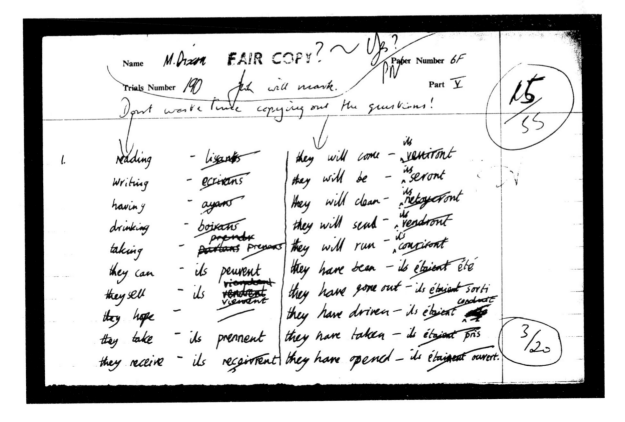

Name *M. Dixon* FAIR COPY? ~ *UB?* Paper Number 6F

Trials Number *190* *Jeb will mark.* Part V

Don't waste time copying out the questions!

15/55

1.	reading	– lisants	they will come –	ils viendront
	Writing	– écrivant	they will be –	ils seront
	having	– ayant	they will clean –	ils nettoyeront
	drinking	– boivant	they will send –	ils vendront
	taking	– ~~parlons~~ prenant	they will run –	ils courront
	they can	– ils peuvent	they have been –	ils étaient été
	they sell	– ils ~~viendent~~ ~~vendent~~ viennent	they have gone out – ils étaient sorti
	they hope	–	they have driven – ils étaient ~~conduit~~
	they take	– ils prennent	they have taken – ils étaient pris
	they receive	– ils reçoivent	they have opened – ils étaient ouvert.

3/20

Tardy book is the traditional punishment given to Etonians for being late. If you are only a couple of minutes late for a *div*, a particularly lenient *beak* might say: "Next time it's *tardy book*, for you." But you will rarely get this second chance. It is the standard punishment for lateness and no one is immune. Even the *Captain of the School* has found himself on *tardy book*.

Once notified of your tardiness, the bureaucracy moves fast. Within twenty-four hours you receive a formal notice saying that for the next five days you are on *tardy book*. Boys who are consistently late usually find it hard to get up early in the morning. For them this is a particularly painful punishment. You have to get into full *school dress*, report at School Office and sign the dreaded book at 7.30 each morning.

To survive at Eton you have to learn a few tricks and I was an old hand at *tardy book*. More than a few times I struggled out of bed at 7.25am, threw my tail coat over my pyjamas, sleep walked the short distance to School Office, and was back in bed in under ten minutes.

It is not advisable to insult *tardy book* by being late for it because it soon bites back. Almost immediately you will find yourself in the hands of its first cousin, *early tardy book*, which is fifteen minutes earlier and fifteen minutes grimmer.

If you stand up *early tardy book* you'll find yourself *on the bill* — face to face with the ultimate authority, the *head man*.

A friend of mine was put on tardy book by his *modern tutor*. Afterwards, the *beak* regretted what he had done but he could not reverse it. So as a compromise the *beak* got up even earlier himself and prepared a cooked breakfast which the boy collected each morning on his way to sign the book.

Etonians are not the only ones punished for being late. The *head man* keeps his eye on *beaks*. If a *beak* arrives for a *div* more than fifteen minutes late, the boys are allowed to take a *run*. They run from the school room to School Office to report the *beak's* tardiness. The *beak* has to write a formal letter of apology to the *head man*. If it happens too often he will find himself on the equivalent of the *bill*.

Captain of the School = The head boy. Tradition goes that he is the only boy who can marry, drive a car and grow a beard while at Eton.

school dress = Eton's black and white uniform, which includes a tail coat, waistcoat, pin striped black trousers, starched collar and white tie.

on the bill = If you are on the *head master's bill*, or *lower master's bill*, you have to appear before one of these figures. In short, it means you are in the soup.

Your *dame* is second in command to your *housemaster* and if you can get her on your side it can be very useful. At times I felt that my *dame* was the only official at Eton who wasn't against me. She would write me excuses for not having done my *E.W.s* on time. She would give me permission to go to Slough. My *housemaster* wrote to my father: "I also like the way in which he invites the *dame* to play table tennis".

The other person you should get on with is your *boy's maid*. One *boy's maid* is shared between fifteen Etonians. She cleans your room but does not make your bed. She washes your dishes but will not make your tea. But the duty she does that is most noticed and least appreciated is waking you up in the morning. My *boy's maid*, Miss Andrews, had held a similar job in the Army and she prided herself on being as tough on us as she had been on them.

Miss Andrews was unrelenting. She launched herself into my room at 7.30 each morning with the same words: "Mornin'. Mornin'. Come on. Get up or I'll chop yer legs off". After saying this to fifteen boys a day for ten years, the phrase became her trademark.

From the Dame,
....K.R.S. (House)

Please excuse...Mark Dixon...
From P.E. to-day. to not
completing his E.W.
owing to severe
toothache &
headache after dental
extraction.
Signed...D.H. Ellam
Date...20/5/78

Mark Dixon
has permission
to go to
Slough
SA. Ellam

A workman draining the *Jordan*.

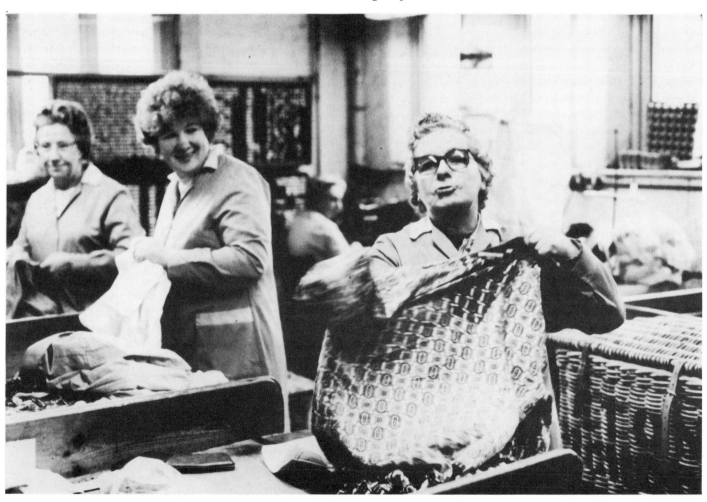

There is one corner of Eton that is rarely seen by boys, *beaks* or even *dames*: the Eton College Laundry. When I visited the laundry ladies with my camera, I was one of the first Etonians they had met. They see the Etonian's laundry but not his face. But they did know my name well — from my Old English name tapes.

In the Michaelmas *half*, an event is arranged that involves *dry bobs*, *wet bobs*, and those who fall in between — the *slack bobs*. This is the six mile *steeplechase*. Even the most devious *slack bob* finds it difficult to escape and for some it might be the only exercise they take in the year. Anyone who doesn't turn up needs to come up with a good excuse and there are only two ways you can do this; either by being ill or persuading your *dame* to say you are ill.

If you are an athlete you will have no trouble completing the course but if you're less nimble the water obstacles can be a problem. The *dry bob* unlucky at one of these might be renamed a *wet bob* for the day. *Slack bobs* are good spectators. One of these, who thought he had avoided participating, was proved wrong when his friends threw him in the *Jordan*, the muddiest of the water hurdles. To make it worse he was wearing his tail coat.

steeplechase = The cross country run.
Jordan = A tributary of the Thames which meanders along the edge of Mesopotamia, one of Eton's playing fields. The jump across the *Jordan* is the hardest water hurdle of the *steeplechase*.

In the *div* before *chambers* a friend might whisper to you behind the *beak's* back or perhaps convey this request scrawled inside a paper dart, "Will you *sock* me at *Rowlands* during *chambers*?". I have to say that it is rare to be on the receiving end of an offer of *socking*.

At *chambers* you have twenty minutes of free time. You might try to complete an *E.W.* at the last minute but you would much prefer to have something to eat. The choice is between going back to you, *house* where *chambers* — a mug of tea or coffee and a bun — is laid on for everyone, or you might race off down the High Street to *Rowlands*.

Until you're eligible for *Tap*, *Rowlands* is probably the place in Eton you'd most like to be. Hot food, ice creams, sweets and chocolate, television, and gossip are all available. I don't think I spent one day at Eton without stopping in at *Rowlands*. Boys rush there between *divs*. It's always a race: getting there, fighting through the crowd, buying what you want and eating it in time to get to the next *div*. There isn't anything like a queue; just a long and very high counter with boys reaching over it, trying to attract the attention of the old girls behind. If they know your face and you know their names you'll be served first. Otherwise you might be waiting there half an hour.

In the Summer *half* you will often hear the words, "Will you *sock* me a Strawberry Mivi★?" or, on colder days, "Will you *sock* me a sausage roll?" And at any time of the year an easy-to-please Etonian might stop you with the words "Come on, don't be so *wet, sock* me something?… Anything?" At this you might be tempted not to understand the Eton language and

thereby justifiably respond with a sock in his face.

In my first *half* someone asked me to *sock* him a *brown cow*. I obliged by ordering one (wondering at the same time if he was pulling my leg). But I soon discovered a *brown cow* was simply a glass of Coca-Cola with a bar of vanilla ice cream floating in it. I have eaten my way through many *brown cows* since. Chips were the rage at *Rowlands*. They cost 14p and you had to pay an extra 1p if you wanted the tomato ketchup. Carol Higham, the manageress, let you pay by cheque if you spent at least 50p. She probably cashed more cheques for boys than all the banks in Eton and launched more banking careers than all the economics *beaks* put together.

The black and white television is the focus of *Rowlands*. When an important football match is on, *Rowlands* is like a stadium complete with football emotions and food fights. 'Doctor Who' on Saturday afternoons got the highest rating. Etonian taste in television can hardly be called highbrow.

★ A Strawberry Mivi was an ice cream with strawberry on the outside and vanilla on the inside, discontinued in the early 1980s.

chambers = The 'elevenses' time when all the *beaks* meet in School Hall, where they are addressed by the *head man*. At this time Etonians are provided with refreshments, also called *chambers*, which are served on the *slab*.

sock = To buy food for another Etonian. The word originates from the "sockads" (meaning sellers of food) who used to congregate at the centre of Eton during the nineteenth century.

wet = Technically it means pathetic, but Etonians also use the word as a general insult.

Once a year, on the Saturday closest to *St. Andrew's Day*, Old Etonians, parents, *beaks*, *dames* and boys all gather with the press corps to watch Eton's strangest sport, the *wall game*. Although the *wall game* is played on most *half holiday* afternoons, the *St. Andrew's Day* match is the only important one and the only one at which the spectators outnumber the players.

Statistically, you are about as likely to get into one of the *wall game* teams as you are to get into *pop*. To get into *College Wall* you have to be very brilliant and to get into the *Oppidan Wall* you just have to be very strong. You might wonder why the *Oppidan Wall* does not always beat the *College Wall*. The reason is that the *Oppidan Wall* has no chance to practise because the *College Wall* owns the pitch.

The two teams form a *bully* and pile up against the *Wall*. It's very difficult to tell whether they are pushing against each other or whether their combined energy is being exerted against the *Wall*. And it is a rare moment if the ball gets any distance from the *Wall* or out of the *bully*. If it does, there is a very small chance that a goal will be scored — a feat which last occurred fifty years ago.

St. Andrew's Day = The Saturday closest to November 30th.
half holiday = The days of the week (Tuesday, Thursday and Saturday) when there are *divs* before, but not after, *boys' dinner*.
College Wall = A *wall game* team made up of *tugs*.
Oppidan Wall = A *wall game* team made up of the strongest *Oppidans*.
bully = A scrum in the *wall game* or *field game*.
Wall = The long, high wall running along the edge of College Field, after which the *wall game* is named.

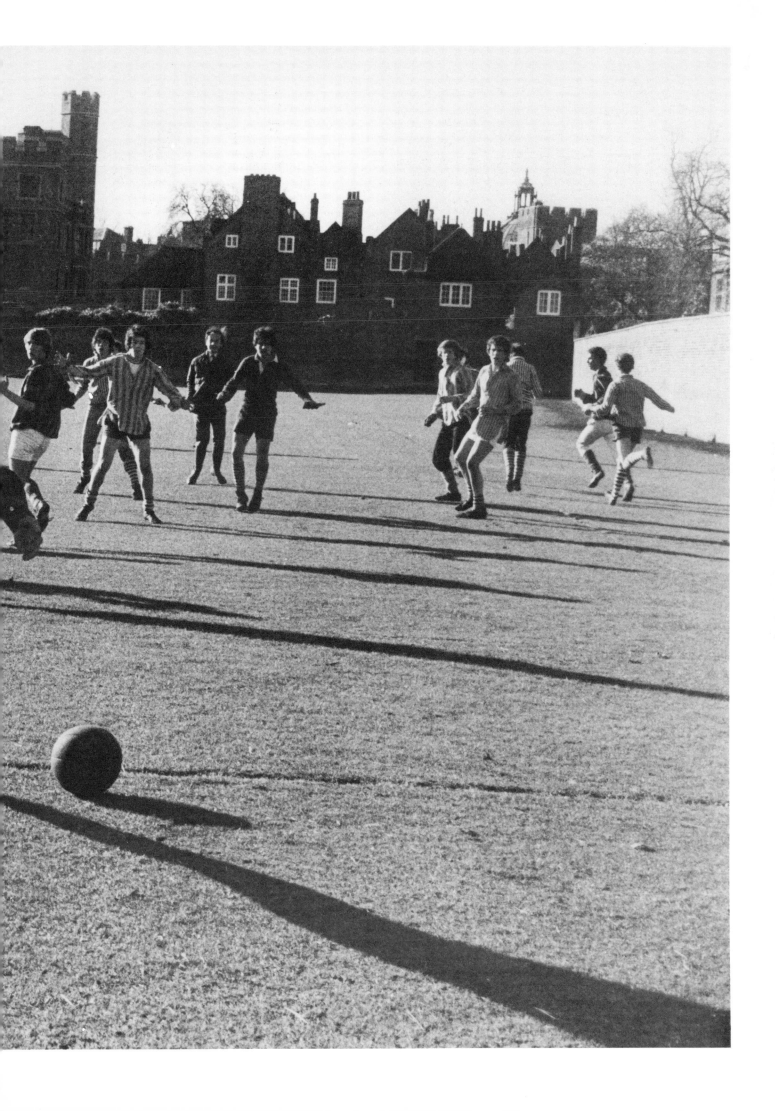

My father (right) with another parent, Nicholas Guppy. He comes from a family of explorers. In 1858, at the age of 21, his grandfather discovered the Guppy fish. Today the Guppy family happen to live in a house called "The Pond".

This is the day when you will find the *provost, vice provost, head master* and *lower master* all in one place; watching the *wall game*. McCrum, the *head man*, austere, distant, but immensely respected, stands with Anderson, the *lower man* (known by the boys simply by his first name, Jack). I am sure Jack was very nice to his wife and children but to us he was petty and officious. Boys would cross the road to avoid him in case he stopped them about the length of their hair or the length of their *tails*. The *provost*, Lord Charteris, formerly the Queen's private secretary, strolls along the muddy touchline supporting neither team and chatting only to the most important parents.

The fathers are telling their sons what Eton was like in their day. The mothers are doing the same. My mother had a lot to say (she is the daughter, sister, wife and mother of Etonians). And the parents without Eton connections feel slightly left out with only the weather to talk about.

provost = Elected by the *fellows,* he is the Chairman of Eton's governing body.
vice provost = The *provost's* deputy, usually a former *housemaster*.
lower master = The *beak* in charge of *lower school* (boys in *E* and *F-blocks*). He is called the *lower man* by the boys.
tails = Tail coat.

The *provost* (left) and the *head man* (right)

The *lower man* walking past my father

Arches, **the viaduct built by the Great Western Railway. When its line was brought through to Windsor, the Act of Parliament obliged the company "to maintain a sufficient additional number of persons for the purpose of preventing and restricting all access to the railway by the scholars of Eton College".**

DIXON! —
YOUR Father
rang to say that
he will not be on
the train at Windsor
station as before but
will meet you at K.R.S.
(rang at 10.55 am)

Tap is the watering hole of Eton. There is strict segregation. Boys are not allowed to visit any other pub and *Tap* is barred to anyone who is not an Etonian or Old Etonian.

The only alcohol served is beer and cider and you're allowed only two pints per day. But that doesn't stop the determined Etonian from spending the whole afternoon in *Tap* and managing to get very drunk. These regulars are called the *Tap bores*.

To be allowed in *Tap* you have to be in *C-block* and over sixteen. On my sixteenth birthday I wasted no time in getting down to *Tap*. The first time it's like entering a busy pub where everyone is a regular except you. And like *Rowlands* the likelihood of your being served depends on how well you know the Smiths.

"Half a pint of your Taunton cider, Mrs. Smith."

"A pint of Newcastle Brown, Mr. Smith."

"What about me, Mr. Smith? I've been waiting here longer. One prawn roll please."

It's not that Etonians are impatient by nature, but there are only twenty minutes at *chambers* and no one is prepared to let someone else be served first if it means getting put on *tardy book*.

Chambers (11.25am to 11.45am) is *Tap's* busiest time of day. Although the two pint ration may teach Etonians to drink in moderation, they certainly get used to drinking fast, and at the wrong time of day.

Apart from an occasional glass of cider, I drank Coca-Cola at *Tap*. Ordering a glass of "Coke" sounded rather dull so instead Mr. Smith and I had our own private language. We used to call it "Vintage". .

Each time I ordered a Vintage, Mr. Smith would respond in the same way. As he poured out a small amount of Coke for me to taste, he would say: "The funny thing about this Vintage stuff, Sir, is that it's almost the same as Coke but slightly more expensive".

C-block = The subdivision of the school consisting of boys who have been at Eton three years.

Above: *College*
Right: my brother with the *Captain of the School*

I was an *oppidan* but my brother was a *tug*. *Tugs*, the scholars of Eton, are its oldest residents, but they have not always been the most comfortable. In 1834 a chronicler wrote: "the inmates of a work-house or gaol are better fed and lodged than the scholars of Eton… They suffer privations that would be thought inhuman if inflicted on a galley slave". There are stories of *tugs* having to supplement their diets by catching rats under the floor boards. But times have changed and my brother found the conditions in *College* rather more comfortable. In his five years he did not eat a single rat.

There is friction between *oppidans* and *tugs*. Most *oppidans* quite wrongly think that *tugs* are only interested in the academic side of life and consequently don't bother to get to know them. *Tugs*, in turn, think *oppidans* are frivolous. They live separately and they have their own traditions — they wear gowns over their *tails* and the letters *K.S.* after their names. Also, and quite unfairly, they are not allowed to invite *oppidans* back to *College* for tea. Entertaining at Eton is a two way street and so *tugs* get left out. But there are some advantages in being a *tug* — apart from the free education, you are surrounded by other brilliant minds and the *Captain of the School* is always selected from your ranks.

College = The *house* where the seventy *tugs* (or *Collegers*) live.
Oppidan = An Etonian who is not a *tug*. The word derives from the Latin *oppidum* meaning town. Originally, the *tugs* lived in the college buildings at the expense of the school and the others lived in boarding houses in the town.

The *Eton Society*, or by its everyday name, *pop*, is a self-elective club of about twenty Etonians. There are a few *ex officio* members★, but most of them are chosen on popularity. They stand out from the black and white surroundings of Eton because of their multi-coloured waistcoats. They are the peacocks of Eton, and its Cabinet.

Some Etonians are transparently out to get into *pop*. No expense is spared. The lobbying takes place in the last year or two when hopeful candidates spend many hours of their free time and most of their allowances buying drinks for existing members in *Tap*. Often their ambitions have been kindled early on in their Eton careers by their contemporaries describing them as *pop material*. It is important not to be seen to be trying to get into *pop*. But this does not stop the ambitious getting their way. They operate with subtlety, always with some change in their pockets and a smile on their faces, making the right friends and not being seen with the wrong people.

Getting into *pop* may not help you much in later life†, but at Eton it is considered the highest achievement. Many Etonians look down on others who excel in academic or sporting fields. The sportsmen call the academics "swots" even if they are not hard-working. And the academics call the sportsmen "rowers", to imply that they are stupid, and they call them this even if they are not *wet bobs*. Those

who excel in both do not escape a label; they are called "too keen". But it is possible to succeed at Eton without being sniped at — by being elected into *pop*. You can find Etonians who will criticize almost anything but I have not yet come across one who would snipe at Popularity.

One boy in his first *half* surprised us all by buttonholing members of *pop* as they sat on *Pop Wall* or as they patrolled the Windsor Bridge. We were even more surprised when we found that, at the end of that *half*, they had given him a huge number of *pop leavers*. But by the end of his career his supporters had long since left and he never made it into their ranks. He had done the right thing at the wrong time.

★ The *ex officio* members of *pop* are the *Captain of the School* and the *Captain of the Oppidans*.

† There are exceptions. A large number of Macmillan's first Cabinet had been in *pop* with him.

pop material = An Etonian thought by his contemporaries to have a chance of getting into *pop*.

swot = An Etonian who studies intensively.

Pop Wall = A wall located in Long Walk, upon which only members of *pop* are allowed to sit.

leaver = A photograph of an Etonian which he gives to his friends when he leaves Eton. He usually adds a short farewell message alongside.

popper = A member of *pop*.

Left: a *popper*

Right: a member of *pop* rehearsing 'Othello'.

Pop is the police force of Eton. If a *popper* spots you violating the dress code, he will fine you with the words: "50p in my room by *lock-up*". He can turn out your pockets in search of cigarettes or alcohol as you return from Windsor. One boy paid a fine by cheque. But he wrote on the back: "I've made it payable to *Tap* because this is where it will be spent." The boy was beaten by the *head man*.

Considered the least burdensome of the *popper's* tasks is what is known as *pop patrol*: a tour of the pubs in Windsor, Slough and Datchet in search of out-of-bounds and rule-breaking Etonians. The British bobby's boast "I never drink on duty" is not heard on this beat because *poppers* enjoy a dispensation from school rules: they are allowed one glass of beer or cider per establishment. In effect, the *pop patrol* is a legalised 'pub crawl'.

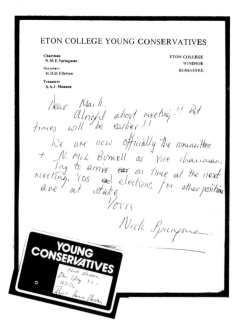

The *beaks*, *dames* and boys are the tour guides of Eton. The Japanese come in the largest numbers. They arrive by the bus-load whatever the weather. They rush out, photographing persistently, as though they expect the penguins to flee. They chase you down the High Street and into New Schools, weighed down by their Nikons, Minoltas, and Yashicas. You learn early in life that Japan is a nation of cameras and that the Japanese are addicted to well-documented information.

Eton does not allow boys to pose for the tourists. You are meant to look away from the camera or raise your school books in front of your face. You may or may not subscribe to the cliché that Eton is good at producing leaders, but certainly Etonians get early instruction in handling a barrage of photographers.

One colleague of mine was approached by a group of Japanese tourists. They wanted to buy his tail coat. He explained that it was against school rules to accept an offer of this kind. They offered him £100 — more than his annual allowance. He handed it over and scarpered down *Judy's Passage* in his shirt-sleeves.

One Eton tour guide ended his tour with the words erroneously attributed to Wellington: "The battle of Waterloo was won in the playing fields of Eton." One puzzled American tourist is said to have complained, "Why didn't they show us Waterloo?"

Another tourist, hearing a passing aeroplane on its way to Heathrow, asked: "Why did they build Eton so close to the airport?"

Judy's Passage = A narrow walled pathway leading from the centre of Eton to a group of boys' *houses*.

My cousin in the centre

When you cross the bridge into Windsor you are in a different world. School rules require you to wear *school dress, half change* or *standard change*. But you will not make more than one trip to Windsor in *school dress*, such is the harrassment that it brings.

Every year Eton makes its own effort to ingratiate itself with the community by arranging a 'Twit of the Year Contest'. Etonians dress up in ridiculous costumes and the locals are encouraged to hurl rotten fruit.

In his second *half* my cousin was thrown into the *Jordan* by two young men from Slough. They gave no reason for their action. Perhaps they were rehearsing the role of Little John in 'Robin Hood'. His favourite green tweed trousers were ruined but his tennis racket survived and he was on the court within half an hour.

half change = The same as *school dress* except that, instead of the tail coat and waistcoat, you wear a sports jacket.
standard change = A jacket and tie. You cannot wear jeans.

The cover I designed for Silver Spoon magazine

When the 'Right to Work March' decided to march through Eton on its way from Merseyside to Westminster we all realised that Eton was not located on the most direct route. The *head man* didn't want the marchers to be provoked by our *tails*. He ordered *standard change* to be worn for the day. Some expected violence. The police were out in force and the media outnumbered them.

When the convoy of lorries arrived at the *Burning Bush* no one got out. There were no rowdy speeches; no stars from the Left. We didn't know what the letters on their banners stood for. Only a few words were exchanged. They looked at us and we looked at them. They didn't like my camera and a few showed it by making rude gestures. But after a couple of minutes the convoy moved on and almost everyone except the *head man* was disappointed.

Burning Bush = The ornate nineteenth century lamp-post in the centre of Eton, which is one of the main meeting places.

Occasionally, perhaps in answer to the persistent prayers of *slack bobs*, the Thames used to burst its banks and drown Eton for several weeks. The *field game*, which is played in rain as well as snow, cannot be played underwater. And those who have bathed in the mud pools of the *wall game* soon discover that there is a maximum water content to the sport. But a flood does not stop one Etonian — the *slack bob*. Delighted at the cancelled games, he wades his way to celebrate at *Rowlands* or *Tap*★.

Sadly, those days of the flood are over. The new flood control system, introduced by the Thames Water Authority, has succeeded. The worst that the elements now inflict on Eton is a heavy blanket of snow.

But while the snow is both welcome and rare, cold weather and dampness are quite the reverse. The generations before us had only two buckets of coal per week. When a contemporary of my father's was at Eton, he astonished a furniture shop on the High Street: each afternoon he would buy a cheap wooden

chair on his father's account. Each evening he would burn it in his fire.

Nowadays, with central heating, a boy's warmth is not dictated by his ingenuity, but by the whim of his *dame*. At the flick of a switch she can turn the *house* into a shivering mass. One of my *beaks* complained to my parents: "[Dixon's] principal activity in school has been to secure himself a place close to the radiator". My brother had chilblains and to fight them he bought a duvet. But the *matron-in-college*† didn't like duvets (she didn't like anything modern). "A duvet will make you sick", she assured him, and it took him a year of campaigning to change her mind.

★ The three arch bridge over the *Jordan* retains the name of the earlier structure — the *Fifteen Arch Bridge* — most of which was swept away in the Great Flood of 1809.

† Naomi Johnson — know by *tugs* as the Battle Axe — has been *matron-in-college* since the Fifties. Her favourite motto, "If you don't eat first course, you can't want second course", didn't wash with the boys.

Judy's Passage

My first (right) and second *housemasters*

Vice provost Coleridge

Eton *beaks* are not expected to mince words.

The first report I got at Eton made a bold prediction: "I have an uncomfortable feeling that he is going to find the academic side of life here something of a struggle."

My *classical tutor* complained that I had "adopted a line of passive resistance to Latin." My academic life did not get off to a glorious start and it was being dragged down particularly by what was nothing short of the haunt of my childhood: *Latin construe* and its various relations. I have always said that my difficulty with Latin was Latin's fault and not mine. It seemed a waste of time. The language is dead. The contortions of its grammar are verging on a joke. I asked my Latin *beak* why every word had to agree with every other word in the sentence. "Because it is a crossword puzzle, Dixon." That did not answer my question. I asked what good it might do me to know a dead language. "A dead language, Dixon? Latin is not dead. Suppose you one day decided to work in the Vatican. How would you fare without it?"

Before my first Summer *half* I was on a *white ticket*. Its colour is not in keeping with its darker side. It is, in fact, the worst academic punishment in the book. A *white ticket* is also a collector's item because they are so rarely issued and they have to be returned to the *head man*. Being on a *white ticket* meant that I was not allowed past Barnes Pool Bridge; that the *lower man* was personally monitoring my progress (this is hardly an honour); and that every one of my *beaks* had to file a special report. My Latin *beak*, "Hatty" Jaques★, came up with the idea that I should experience the *white ticket*. But my gating did not prevent me from enjoying myself for the simple reason that *Rowlands* was on my side of the Barnes Pool Bridge.

★ A boy in "Hatty" Jaques's *house* — "Hatty" was almost entirely bald — shaved off his hair to win a £50 wager from his friends. *On the bill*, he was told by the *head man* that he would be expelled unless he wore a toupé. The boy did buy a toupé but it was a very scanty one, closely resembling his *housemaster's* own hair style.

"Hatty" Jaques

CONSTRUE

H.P. Dixon

1. Clusium. ✓
2. of the same ..... ✓
3. This ✗
4. The senators were not only frightened by the enemy, but also their own citizens.   3
5. Congero - I grant, I give. |
6. nice - things. ✗
7. Dat. flumine. total. ✗
8. Wood. ✓
9. By chance. ✓
10. Smaller. ✗   8
                         15

A narrow pass

Check it carefully

---

grief   DIXON

When Caesar Augustus was emperor, it is said that a dolphin was very fond of the son of a poor man, who used to feed him on scraps of bread. Daily the dolphin, having been called by the boy swam to the surface, and carried him from the shore of Baiarae to his school at Puteoli in clothes and brought him back at night in the evening. However after a few months the boy died, and the dolphin after frequent visits to the usual spot is said to have himself died of grief.

F 11   Final Order - Summer

	Latin (479)	Lit. Subjects (507)	Total (986)
1. Fortescue	1	5=	732
2. W. Johnson	3	4	699
3. J. Graham mi	5	3	693
=4. N. Gibbs	12=	1	679
Sheepshanks	2	18	679
6. Huxley	6	16	668
7. Fane mi	8	7	667
8. A. Bailey	4	20	664
9. Akroyd	7	13=	663
10. Long	9=	8=	657
11. Raben	9=	11=	656
12. Cunningham-Reid	11	8=	655
13. W. Farmer	12=	15	653
14. Woodward	18	2	652
15. G. Scott	15	8=	645
16. Keate	16	13=	641
17. Le Roux	19	5=	634
18. Leatham	20	17	618
19. Lord Durham	12=	21	615
20. Johnston mi	21	11=	609
21. Browning	17	22	600
22. Dixon	(22	19	582)

Average Age (July) 13.8

July   K. J. T. Jaques

... F ... DIXON
_____

Poor Work

... a White Ticket from 28 May
KRS (Please report on him in 4 Tues) 15 June

SIGNATURE			REMARKS
House Tutor KRS	////	////	... father ... to be ... ... new Effort
Classical Tutor PN	✓ ✓	✓ ✓	...
Division Master WJN	K ✓✓✓	K ✓✓✓	Better
Form	JWL		
Math	KAH	✗	Low marks but ... hard.
...	...	✗	Satisfactory ...

Left: *vice provost* Macindoe
Right: Tony Butler, my *modern tutor*

Below right: "Nutty" Routledge
Below: "Larry" Jarrett

A boy and a *beak* playing a practical joke on the school

FORTNIGHTLY ORDERS

Name: Dixon   Division: F II

Imagines his... on his... PW

I.		II.		III.	
22 / 22	151 / 276	21 / 22	138 / 237	13 / 22	156 / 231

Thoroughly LAZY in my opinion. PW

I. Latin 21 English 20
Plenty of ideas and theories. But he must learn properly.

II. Latin 21 English 21
Not yet properly serious. How serious? ?

III. Latin 16 English 7=
The treatment has begun to work. Good. Continue. PW

IV.		V.		VI.	
21 / 22	37 / 2+2	22 / 22	582 / 986		

IV. Latin 2= English in 4=
...

V. Latin 22 English 19

N 111

When my period on the *white ticket* was over, everyone stepped forward with their own comments. "Hatty" himself said that my "spell on the *white ticket* seemed salutary". My French beak explained: "I fear that we must accept that he was misplaced in this *division*… and he has clearly been floundering." My *housemaster* came up with a very novel excuse to my father: "This excessive heat affects people in different ways, and perhaps it may have affected Mark more than others." But my father had his own theory and wrote so in reply to Mr. Spencer: "It was generous of you to suggest that his poor performance during the *half* might have been explained by the hot weather… [but] I think one of the problems is that he has always had a bad memory." They had all been generous but they had all got the wrong reason. It was my photography.

My English *beak*, an Australian, however, was more content: "[Dixon] gave a short talk on 'Kangaroos' and spoke with considerable poise." But Latin never saw any progress: "The figures and gap between Dixon and the next lowest boy… underline just how far behind he has been." The following *half* the same *beak* added, with considerable artistic license: "Organisation was Dixonian. *Order cards* and textbooks disappeared, were stolen by Japanese tourists or accidentally put in the toaster."

As soon as I entered *D-block* Latin became voluntary. I was relieved. My *classical tutor* thought it fitting to conclude: "Dixon has hardly finished his career as my pupil in a blaze of glory." And my physics *beak* added: "The standard of the *division* was not very high, and he had no difficulty in coming bottom of it."

order card = A report on your academic performance each month.
D-block = The subdivision of the school consisting of boys who have been at Eton two years.

The theory goes that in the Summer *half* the school splits into two groups: the *dry bobs* and the *wet bobs*. In practice there is also a third group — the *slack bobs*.

In my first Summer *half* I didn't know about this third category and so I had to choose between cricket and rowing. I had hated the hot afternoons that came with cricket at my private school, where as a wicket-keeper I had more than once begun to doze off, only to be awoken by a cricket ball. On the other hand, I associated rowing with an afternoon on the Serpentine in Hyde Park — an entirely voluntary activity. And the flexibility of the *wet bobs* schedule suited my photographic career. It was not, therefore, with any prospect of second thoughts that I told the *Captain of Games* that I would join the large contingent of *wet bobs* in our *house*.

Although *dry bobs* do occasionally take *gigs* out on the river, *wet bobs* never play cricket. So once I had decided to be a *wet bob* I thought I had escaped cricket for the rest of my life. But the *Chronicle* had other plans for me and posted me to *Agar's Plough*, Eton's main cricket pitch. After a couple of hours under the sun I realised why the boys I was photographing were called *dry bobs*. Not all *dry bobs* are *dry bobs* by choice. If a *wet bob* fails his swimming test he is forced by school rules to become a *dry bob*.

Captain of Games = The boy in each *house* in charge of sports.
gig = A wide boat used by *dry bobs* because it is almost impossible to capsize.

The Eton-Winchester match and the Eton-Harrow match are the two main cricket events of the year. When the Winchester match is played at Winchester the whole school turns up to watch. It is their equivalent of the *Fourth of June*. But when it is played at home Etonians don't bother to watch.

The Wykehamists are furious because the Etonians are much more interested in the Eton-Harrow match at Lords.

Fourth of June = Eton's sports day.

Wet bobs always talk about Eton's small island on the Thames in the direction of Maidenhead. It is called Queen's Eyot and a short row there seemed a lazy way to spend my first afternoon on the river. Queen's Eyot offers more than just a resting place to the weary rower: beer, cider and four different types of potato crisps are in plentiful supply. I was developing a taste for cider. I thought it would be nice to pursue this a little further and at Queen's Eyot any *wet bob* can drink, regardless of his age.

Queen's Eyot doesn't look far on a map, but in an ageing *rigger* it's quite a trip. And it takes even longer when you are a first day *wet bob*. When the Thames meanders, you have to meander, even if you haven't mastered which oar turns you in which direction. If you're on the wrong side of the river a passing eight might hole you in seconds. Even if you're on the correct side of the river there are still the tourist motor cruisers which don't always observe river etiquette. If one of these runs into you, your vessel is much more likely to sink than theirs. I remembered Nanny's story of my uncle's narrow escape at Romney Weir and this took away the relaxed spirit with which I had started the journey.

But within three hours I was being helped out of my *rigger* at Queen's Eyot. It hadn't been the lazy afternoon that I had expected and, as I sat down with a glass of cider, I realised why there was no need to ration the alcohol at Queen's Eyot: it was such a long way to row home drunk.

rigger = The type of sculling boat used by first year *wet bobs*.

Left: the *Captain of the School* in his *Monarch* colours
Below: *Rafts*

A *wet bob*, a *dry bob* and a *slack bob*

The biggest excitement of the rowing season is the week of the *bumping fours*. Each *house* provides a four (four rowers and a cox). The teams are arranged in heats and positioned a little distance apart along the river. The aim is to bump the boat in front of you and not be bumped by the boat behind you. A *double bump* is when the boat in front bumps the boat two boats in front of you and you bump the boat three boats ahead. Most of the school turns up for these races and it's one of the only times you'll see *dry bobs* near the river, as they cluster together in their cricket colours feeling slightly left out but cheering on their own teams anyway. I overheard one *dry bob* say: "What a silly sport — they're pointing in one direction and going in the other."

By the time my second Summer *half* came around I had learnt what a *slack bob* was and I promptly became one. A *slack bob* is officially a *wet bob*, who pays the rent for the boat to make it official, but who doesn't go near the river. If you're a *slack bob* you might get away with as little as a game of *fives* or an occasional set of tennis. I always maintained that photography was my sport. But while being a *slack bob* may be easy on the heart it does not carry much cachet at Eton. You can escape the *slack bob* label by keeping yourself busy doing academic work, but in that case you will almost certainly be branded a *swot*, which is worse.

My mother, brother and Patrick Morin, a friend from America.

The Fourth of June is Eton's big day and one of England's biggest drinks parties. The champagne pops at 9.30 in the morning (as soon as you are out of Chapel) and it flows until *absence* is read at 5.30pm.

Hardly anyone remembers what Eton is celebrating on *The Fourth* — George III's birthday. He and Henry VI were the only two monarchs who loved Eton. Etonians are encouraged to overlook the fact that they were also England's only two mad monarchs. But that didn't stop George III from interrupting his conversations with the trees in Windsor Great Park to stroll down the High Street and chat with Etonians between *divs*.

Some parents rent a 'Rolls' for the day. Others leave the 'Rolls' behind in case it would embarrass their son, and rent a 'Mini' instead.

The day is packed with things to do. Every Etonian buys a carnation for his buttonhole. There are picnics on the playing fields, mothers' hats to laugh at, and friends' sisters to flirt with. There are *housemasters'* drinks parties (for parents). For the academically inclined there is *Speeches* in Upper School, where members of *sixth form select* show their oratorical skills. When my brother was in *sixth form select* he surprised the crowd by his choice of Pericles's *Funeral Oration* which he delivered in Ancient Greek. There were only a few Classical scholars who could understand him, but the rest were entertained by his impersonation of Pericles.

The Fourth = The everyday name for the *Fourth of June*.

sixth form select = A group of the twenty leading scholars in the sixth form chosen on purely academic grounds according to their *trials* performance over the years. Their number is usually made up of ten *K.S.s* and ten *O.S.s*, including the *Captain of the School* and the *Captain of the Oppidans*.

BUCKINGHAM PALACE
2th September, 1976

Princess Anne
has asked me to write and thank you
for your letter and the photograph.

The Princess
thought it was most kind of you to send
this to her and I am to send to you her
most sincere thanks.

Yours sincerely,

Lady in Waiting to
HRH The Princess Anne,
Mrs. Mark Phillips.

Mark Dixon, Esq.

For the *dry bobs*, and the fathers who were *dry bobs* in their day, the high point of the day is the cricket match: Eton versus *The Ramblers*. For the *wet bobs* there is the *Procession of Boats*. As each boat passes the crowd it attempts a stunt. First the cox stands up. Then slowly raising his oar perpendicular to the water each oarsman gets to his feet. The band strikes up the Eton Boating Song and flowers fall from the oarsmen's boaters as they take off their hats and shake them over the water.

At 5.30pm *absence* is read to make sure that no boy has left early. But it would be very strange for anyone to miss *The Fourth of June*. After *absence* everyone tries to leave Eton at the same time. The hooting of horns of those who are impatient at Eton's annual traffic jam mixes with the chitter-chatter and popping corks of those who are not.

The Ramblers = A cricket team made up of Old Etonians.

If you have done something wrong and you get caught, you will be *on the head master's bill*, or, as is more often said, *on the bill*. You will usually first hear of your appointment with the *head man* during the *div* directly after *chambers*.

Your formal summons will often take place while the *beak* taking your *div* is half-way through some lengthy dissertation. The door of the school room is flung open by a *praepostor*. He will be wearing the full uniform of *sixth form select: stick ups*, silver buttons on his braided waistcoat, and, if he's a *tug* member, he will also sport a gown.

"Is Dixon *Ma* in this *division?*" The *praepostor* is not required to wait for the *beak* to come to the end of his sentence. As ambassador of the *head man*, he has important business to execute and politeness is not expected.

It is for the *beak* and not the boy to reply. If the answer is, "yes", the *praepostor* will continue, "He is to see the *head master, on the bill*, at 1.05 today." Without a goodbye, or so much as a nod of the head, the *praepostor* slams the door behind him and moves on to summon the next criminal.

praepostor = From the Latin *praepositor* meaning an overseer.

stick-ups = White bow tie and wing collar. Worn by Etonians who have succeeded, in one of a variety of different ways.

Ma = Short for *Major*, the elder of two brothers. The younger brother is called *Mi*, for *Minor*.

When I stood in front of the *head man* he didn't look pleased. I had organized a petition amongst the boys to save the lot of Eric, the ice cream man. His future at Eton had been threatened by some senior *beaks* who were trying to arrange his removal from the High Street.

"We don't like round robins at Eton, Dixon. We don't like them at all." He was speaking to me and to the next four who signed my petition. If he had put all the signatories *on the bill* his office would have been crammed with close to three hundred Etonians.

I didn't know what a round robin was, so I thought it best to ask.

"This is a round robin", he said, holding up my five sheets of cardboard entitled "Who wants Eric at Eton?". He told me that I was a subversive element. I replied that I didn't think my petition was subversive; it was taken on the High Street in broad daylight and it was to be handed in to the authorities. So it was "SUPRA-versive" I politely suggested. The *head man* couldn't argue with my Latin and he let us go without punishment.

The punishments at Eton vary between type and source. The *head man* and *lower man* are the only two who are allowed to beat boys. And both have a large assortment of other punishments to choose from.

The shortest *georgic* is more than five hundred lines of Latin verse which you have to copy out word for word, regardless of whether you are still studying this ancient language. The *head man* might inflict several of these.

If he thinks you need some fresh air he may give you an afternoon of *moss picking*. You report to School Office at the appointed hour. The School Clerk gives you a small cushion and a scraping instrument. You walk into School Yard, kneel on the cushion amongst the flint stones and begin scraping away the chunks of moss. Your back will soon begin to ache. If there are any puddles around, and there usually are in School Yard, the cushion will absorb them. You wonder why they don't use waterproof cushions, and then you remember — it's a punishment you're doing. Weed-killer would do the trick on the moss, but the head gardener would not dare to make the suggestion. The only afternoon I spent *moss picking* was not very painful. I persuaded the School Clerk to give me two cushions. This was an unusual request but there was no rule against it. He showed me the territory I was to crawl over and soon my brother arrived. He sat on one cushion and I knelt on the other, chatting and scraping moss. It was much more fun than an afternoon of Latin.

georgic = The word comes from Virgil's poem on farming called the *'Georgics'*, which he wrote in 30 B.C.

Eton College

SCHOOL RULES: GENERAL PRINCIPLES

The *School Rules* are not intended as a complete guide to conduct, but for guidance on certain details. They are reviewed regularly and kept to the minimum necessary for the safety, welfare, good order, and convenience, of the majority.

In general no boy shall say or do anything contrary to good order, decency, or common sense. Boys are expected to show courtesy and respect for other people at all times, and a proper regard for the reputation of the School.

Failure to observe these general principles will be regarded as a breach of School discipline.

These Rules (together with any additional regulations which may be issued from time to time) apply in Eton during the whole of each half, including the days on which the School opens and closes; to teams, groups, or individuals, who are away from Eton during the half; at Corps camps; on public transport when leaving or returning to Eton. They may be amended as required and with such amendments continue to apply so long as a boy remains a pupil in the School, irrespective of his age.

Revised January 1975

M. McCRUM
Head Master

Name DIXON MA   Paper Number

Trials Number   Part

P. VERGILI MARONIS
GEORGICON
LIBER I

Quid faciat laetas segetes, quo sidere terram
uertere, Maecenas, ulmisque adiungere uitis
conueniat, quae cura boum, qui cultus habendo
sit pecori, apibus quanta experientia parcis,
hinc canere incipiam. uos o clarissima mundi
lumina, labentem caelo quae ducitis annum;
Liber et alma Ceres, uestro si munere tellus
Chaoniam pingui glandem mutauit arista,
poculaque inuentis Acheloia miscuit uuis;
et uos, agrestum praesentia numina, Fauni
(ferte simul Faunique pedem Dryadesque puellae:
munera uestra cano); tuque o, cui prima frementem
fudit equum magno tellus percussa tridenti,
Neptune; et cultor nemorum, cui pinguia Ceae
ter centum niuei tondent dumeta iuuenci;
ipse nemus linquens patrium saltusque Lycaei
Pan, ouium custos, tua si tibi Maenala curae
adsis, o Tegeaee, fauens, oleaeque Minerua
inuentrix, uncique puer monstrator aratri,
et teneram ab radice ferens, Siluane, cupressum:
dique deaeque omnes, studium quibus arua tueri,
quique nouas alitis non ullo semine fruges
quique satis largum caelo demittitis imbrem,
tuque adeo, quem mox quae sint habitura deorum
concilia incertum est, urbisne inuisere, Caesar,
terrarumque uelis curam, et te maximus orbis

Moss picking is considered a rather degrading experience and one of my contemporaries was interrupted by an inquisitive tourist. He wanted to know why an Etonian was on his hands and knees amongst the puddles. The boy answered: "Only members of my family are allowed to pick the moss in School Yard and every morning I come here to exercise my ancestral rights."

Housemasters and *beaks* can give their own punishments but for a serious crime (such as smoking or drinking alcohol) the *housemaster* is obliged to send you to the *head man*. In these cases there is room for negotiation with your *housemaster*: he knows you don't want to be sent to the *head man*, but you know that won't look good for his *house* and his management of it. Cases of smoking and drinking are often therefore settled 'out of court'.

When my *housemaster* retired, his friend, Mr. Haddon, took over. My father wrote to the latter: "I certainly would wish to be counted among the parents who would like to see greater discipline in the wider sense of that word."

Poppers also get a chance to punish Etonians. It is left to them to enforce the dress code. Unless you are a member of *pop* you are not allowed to have your umbrella fastened. The bottom button of your waistcoat must be left undone and if you're showing a *white triangle* you will not long go unnoticed.

white triangle = A *white triangle* exists when your white shirt can be seen under the 'V' of your waistcoat.

The *Chronicle* is Eton's fortnightly magazine. Edited by one *tug* and one *oppidan*, it has something for everyone. The leaders are read by the intellectuals. The sports section caters to both *wet bobs* and *dry bobs* and there is even a gossip column for the *slack bobs*.

When I arrived at Eton, my highest ambition was to get a photograph published in the *Chronicle*. By the end of my career, when my brother had become an editor, I was desperate to rid myself of *Chronicle* assignments.

The *Chronicle's* most regular subscribers are other newspapers. Every national newspaper uses the *Chronicle* for fill-in stories and most manage to find something controversial to quote. One *Chronicle* leader sparked off the Eton Apathy Debate, which became front page news. A letter to the editor from a boy complaining that the laundry had over-starched his collars was taken up by the tabloids.

Free press does not exist at Eton because the *head man*, or his deputy, often censors articles. But the *head man* is not all powerful and once, in response to a joint letter from the *Keeper of the College Wall* and the *Keeper of the Oppidan Wall*, he had to apologize for his earlier derogatory comments about the *wall game*.

Keeper of the College Wall = Captain of the *College Wall*.
Keeper of the Oppidan Wall = Captain of the *Oppidan Wall*.

Right: a first proof of the *Chronicle* is examined by the two editors

You will find graffiti on the bathroom walls, scratched into the desks and walls of the school rooms and into the pews of *College Chapel* as well as on the covers and insides of the textbooks, and just about anywhere in Eton where there is a flat surface.

Some graffiti have not changed from one generation to the next. The cover of 'The Shorter Latin Primer', a text on Latin grammar published in 1843 and used at Eton since 1866, has over the years consistently been altered to 'The Shortbread Eating Primer'. It is, in fact, almost impossible to find an undefaced copy of this book in school bounds. Even if you do have your own copy, and have resisted the temptation to deface it yourself, you will find that someone else soon obliges.

There is one form of graffiti of which Eton approves. These are the early Eton graffiti, some dating back to the early sixteenth century. Famous Etonians, who left their engravings in the panels of Upper and Lower School, include Walpole, Fox and Gladstone. Shelley carved his name twice. While a tour guide proudly shows his flock of German, Japanese and, occasionally, plain English tourists these examples of graffiti by long since dead Etonians, a stone's throw away a modern day Etonian is being caught and punished for just the same crime.

In 1977 one boy spray-painted a *'smiley'* on the outside wall of School Hall. He was never caught but a few days later in *head master's assembly*, the *head man* made this plea: "If you do have to paint smiley faces on our buildings, please refrain from doing so in indelible paint." My father's *head man*, addressing boys on their departure in the late 1940s, said: "If you do have to commit adultery, please refrain from doing so in an Old Etonian dressing gown."

Graffiti, vandalism and pranks are frequent but that doesn't stop them from being at the centre of conversation. A red pyramid was constructed over the *Burning Bush* to commemorate the Queen's Silver Jubilee. This was destroyed by three O.E.s on the eve of the *Fourth of June*. One group of boys painted a zebra

crossing outside *Lower Chapel* so that they would have priority in their last minute dash to Chapel. The boy who climbed the dome of School Library to leave a yellow dustbin perched on the cupola on the eve of *St. Andrew's Day* was caught and *rusticated*. Once a group of boys winched a car to the roof of School Hall. And whoever it was who left a path of 'pink panther' footsteps along *Judy's Passage* has not yet been exposed by his Clouseau.

Someone objected to the activities of the Eton College Beagling Club and left this entirely factual statement on the wall of School Hall: "Eton College Kills Hares".

'smiley' = ☺.

head master's assembly = An occasion every few weeks when *Upper School* assembles to hear the *head man*.

rusticate = To expel from Eton on a temporary basis, usually for the remainder of the *half*.

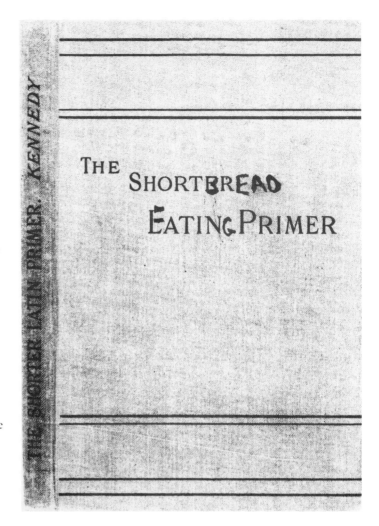

Michael Kidson, my history *beak*

My great-great-great-great uncle's claim to fame was that he had Gladstone as his *fag*. Our family does not record how well he served in that capacity but it is known that, by the end of his Eton career, he had achieved prominence as an orator. In his first speech to *pop*, which in his day was the debating society, he proposed the motion that "Education is on the whole good for the poor". Forty-five years later, when Prime Minister, he introduced free education. Perhaps his *fag master* had taught him to practise what he preached.

If you count Britain's Prime Ministers from Walpole to the present day, you will find that eighteen out of forty-five were Old Etonians. Only two of them were *tugs*. One third of Mrs. Thatcher's first Cabinet were O.E.s as are about seventy of Britain's M.P.s.

Walpole's father got him a scholarship by lying about his age. Macmillan (or "Goofy Macmillan" as he was called) was also a *tug*. Shelley had two nicknames: "Mad Shelley" and "Shelley the Atheist". The teasing that he suffered, which was considerable, may have given him extra drive, and it certainly could not have held him back. Before *taking leave*, his Gothic horror novel *Zastrozzi* was already for sale in the High Street bookshop. There is a story of the day when his *housemaster* irritated him by not knocking on his door before entering. Shelley connected some acid batteries to the brass door handle so that, on his next visit, his *housemaster* was welcomed by a powerful electric shock.

Despite Lord Home's success at Eton — he was *President of Pop* — his contemporary, Cyril Connolly, said of him in 1938: "In the eighteenth century he would have become Prime Minister before he was thirty; as it was he appeared honourably ineligible for the struggle of life". Thirty-five years later Home became Prime Minister.

Not all Etonians who found success in later life were successful or happy in their Eton days. Arthur Wellesley, who became the first

Lord Home

Duke of Wellington, was miserable. His parents had to take him away at the age of fifteen.

Lord Randolph Churchill was so unhappy at Eton that he sent his son Winston to Harrow. But Winston didn't like Harrow and *his* son, Randolph, went back to Eton.

Even Eton's infamous offspring have their supporters. Burgess's *housemaster*, Mr. Dobbs, went to the grave protesting his pupil's innocence, even though the evidence was irrefutable. Such is the blind faith of an Eton *housemaster*.

taking leave = An appointment with the *head man* at the end of your Eton career.

President of Pop = The *President of Pop* is elected by the other members of *pop*. He meets regularly with the *head man* to discuss *pop's* responsibilities.

a classic →

Mark,
thankyou
for years of superb
photos, for plays,
leavers, Chronicle
and divers other
occasions.
Thankyou for your sharp tongue and wicked
eye, your scheming mind and sense of the
absurd. Thankyou for always having time to
listen to others and to take an interest.
— truly creative : TO BEAT BEATON ???
love, Rory

At the turn of the century my great-grandfather, Shirley Atchley, was a photographer with the English Photographic Company in Athens★. Everyone at Eton knew me as a photographer. Most of my money went on photography and most of it came from photography. The photographic shop in Windsor probably thought I had a huge allowance from my parents and the leaving boys who commissioned me to do their *leavers* must have thought I was growing rich on them. In fact my expenses equalled my income with the help of two balancing items: Coca-Cola and brie.

Leavers are always ordered at the most inconvenient time — at the end of the *half*, just when you're meant to be revising for *trials*. But business was business and, when I wasn't at *Rowlands*, I could be found in my room, which I had converted into a makeshift darkroom.

While most boys were doing their *E.W.s* or *swotting* for *trials*, I was printing *leavers* late into the night. Having your lights on after *lights out* (10pm) is a serious offence and most boys either comply or suffer the discomfort of trying to write an essay under the sheets in flickering torchlight. Monks must have found it easier to work by candlelight. But *lights out* suited me fine. My lights were out long before 10pm and production from the darkroom continued long after.

★ Atchley took the standard photograph of Hermes of Praxiteles, which was used on Crete's first postage stamp.

My brother's *leaver*

I usually visited the camera shop wearing *half change*...

Mark Pierson Dixon

PHOTOGRAPHER

With Compliments

Mr Spencer

Apart from producing *leavers* and working for the *Chronicle's* gossip column, I also had a business in passport photographs. My first *housemaster*, Mr. Spencer, was one of my first customers. He wrote to my father: "I am grateful to him for assisting photographically in getting my new passport. I am not sure that I found the result flattering, but then passport photographs seldom are".†

If you want an intensive business course at Eton you could do no better than get into the *leaver* business. You will see fierce competition: price cutting in an efficient and sensitive market. Sometimes a few of the big producers form an oligopoly. You have to meet production deadlines on time because, if you don't, you'll find your customers have left the school. You also have to pay tax if you use the Photographic Society darkrooms because they have a *leaver* levy.

The customer calls the shots. Some want to pose in their favourite outfit. Others will take you in search of a brick wall where only the horizontal lines show. Some want to be recorded at the entrance to *Judy's Passage* or in mid-air after jumping off the *Wall*. And some insist on being photographed bicycling in their favourite river.

† Mr. Spencer was unaware of John Train's Rule of Passports: "If you look like your passport photograph, you're too sick to travel".

Mark –
Thanks for all the photos of various kinds – You must be bored stiff of this face of mine after producing so many copies of it. You and your brother make a superb duo
Philip

Dixon – Can you take photos of as many of the following as possible for the chronicle gossip column by Tuesday p.m. – Parham KS
Harley ma DNC (legs only, please)
Uniacke FPEG
Cohen JWT

Can you also get some pictures of the XI playing today? Thank you very much
Guy Philipps (USI)

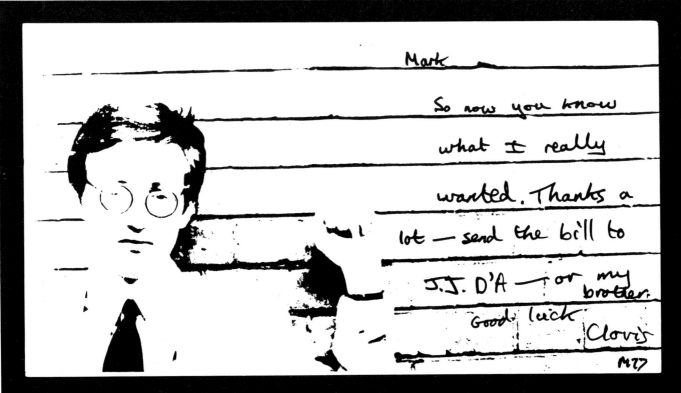

Mark

So now you know
what I really
wanted. Thanks a
lot — send the bill to
J.J. D'A — or my brother.
Good luck
Clovis

M27

Taking leave must be a different experience for every Etonian. You may be as relieved as a prisoner just unshackled. Or you might be unsure of how you are going to fare in the big wide world beyond. My farewell appointment with the *head man* came upon me rather fast. I had been doing my own *leavers* as well as others and in the rush I stood up the *head man*. He may have wanted to put me on *tardy book* but we both knew I wouldn't have signed it if he had. Instead, another appointment was arranged.

It was a very strange feeling to be standing in front of a smiling headmaster because I had never seen one smile at me before. And it was only then that I fully realised that my Eton career was nearly over. This world that I had lived in for five years would soon become history. The *beak* I had feared only a few days before was about to become just a man with a job.

When the *head man* asked me his standard question, "What did you enjoy most at Eton?", I didn't know whether to tell him or not.

After a brief pause I replied.

"Photography, Sir".

Taking leave = Some Etonians in effect never *take leave*. After three years at Oxford or Cambridge they return as *beaks*, later to become *housemaster*. Fred Coleridge continued up the ladder to become *vice provost*. It is said that the *Captain of the School* never has to *take leave*.

The Eton Language

absence: a roll call taken by *housemasters* at 8.30pm each
evening. In the Summer *half* there is also a 5.30pm *absence*.

Agar's Plough: Eton's main cricket pitch.

Arches: the viaduct built by the Great Western Railway.
When its line was brought through to Windsor, the Act of
Parliament obliged the company "to maintain a sufficient
additional number of persons for the purpose of
preventing and restricting all access to the railway by the
scholars of Eton College".

beak: master. Like *tugs* every *beak* wears a gown. You must
refer to a *beak* as "Sir", and if you walk past him on the
street you must also *cap* him.

Bekynton: the central feeding complex, where about ten
houses are fed. It is named after Bishop Bekynton, Henry
VI's secretary.

bill: see *on the bill*.

boy call: a yell by a member of *library* summoning all *fags* to
the *library*.

boys' dinner: lunch.

boy's maid: the maid who assists about fifteen Etonians with
their cleaning

brown cow: a glass of Coca-Cola with a bar of vanilla ice
cream floating in it, available at Rowlands. When I
arrived at Eton, a *brown cow* cost 15p.

bully: a scrum in the *field game* or *wall game*.

bumping fours: an annual rowing race involving every *house*.

Burning Bush: the ornate nineteenth-century lamp-post in
the centre of Eton which is one of the main meeting
places.

C-block: the subdivision of the school consisting of boys
who have been at Eton three years.

C-Sunday: a Sunday morning service in *College Chapel*, at
which Holy Communion is celebrated.

cap: to raise your right index finger to where the rim of your
top hat would be if you were wearing one. Top hats were
dropped from *school dress* at the beginning of the last war.
Boys had to carry gas masks and there were not enough
hooks outside *Chapel* for top hats as well.

Captain of Games: the boy in each *house* in charge of sports.

Captain of the Eleven: captain of Eton's top football team.

Captain of the Oppidans: the boy appointed head of the
oppidans by the *head man*.

Captain of the School: the head boy. He is always selected
from the *tugs*. According to tradition, he is the only boy
who can marry, drive a car and grow a beard while at
Eton. He also has the privilege of never having to *take
leave*.

chambers: 1 The 'elevenses' time (11.25am to 11.45am) when
all the *beaks* meet in School Hall to be addressed by the
head man. At this time Etonians are provided with
refreshments, which are served on the *slab*.
2 *Chambers* also refers to the refreshments
themselves.

Chronicle: The Eton College Chronicle is a fortnightly
magazine edited by an *oppidan* and a *tug*.

classical tutor: the *beak* who looks after your academic life
until you are sixteen.

clothes' list: the very long list of clothes which every *new boy*
has to arrive with. It includes twelve handkerchiefs and
two tail coats.

College: the *house* where the seventy *tugs* (or collegers) live.

College Chapel: Eton's main chapel, erected by Henry VI in
1441. He laid the foundation stone on Passion Sunday.

colleger: Tug.

College Wall: a *wall game* team made up of *tugs*.

colours' test: a test given to *new boys* after three weeks at Eton.
It covers the school and *house* colours; Eton's history,
geography and language.

commended for good effort: a paper reward given to a boy who
has shown improvement. It is shown to the *head man*, his
housemaster and *classical tutor* or *modern tutor*.

Common Entrance: the standard exam adopted by most
public schools.

conduct: Eton's senior chaplain.

construe (v): to translate from Latin into English.

construe (n): see *Latin construe*.

construe test: in a *construe test* any boy can be called upon to
translate from Latin out loud.

cornering: a foul in the *field game*.

D-block: the subdivision of the school consisting of boys
who have been at Eton two years.

D-worship: a special daily assembly for the boys in *D-block*,
who are considered too unruly to send to Chapel every
day.

dame: the matron in each *house*. It is a prime job for a spinster
who wishes to have a lot of children. You must refer to
her as "Ma'am".

debate: the governing body of each *house* under the *library*. It
consits mainly of boys in *C-block*.

div: abbreviation for *division*.

division: 1 a lesson.
2 a class of boys.

double bump: the ambition of every oarsman in the *bumping
fours*.

dry bob: a cricketer.

E-block: the subdivision of the school consisting of boys who
have been at Eton one year.

E.W.: abbreviation for *extra work*, meaning home work.

early tardy book: a punishment given to Etonians for missing
tardy book.

Eton Society: pop, the self-elective club of Eton.
extra work: homework.

F-block: the subdivision of the school consisting of boys in their first year.
fag: an Etonian who acts as servant to another Etonian.
fagging: serving another Etonian. Fagging was recently abolished.
fag master: an Etonian who has a *fag* to serve him.
fellows: the governing body of Eton.
Field: Eton's top *field game* team.
field game: Eton's home-grown combination of soccer and Rugby football, played with a round ball. The rules were set in 1847. Eton is the only place where it is played.
Fifteen Arch Bridge: the three arch bridge over the *Jordan* retains the name of the earlier structure, most of which was swept away in the great flood of 1809.
fives: similar to squash, but played with the hands instead of a racket. There are two theories of how *fives* got its name: the nineteenth century slang for 'hands' was 'fives', as in "I must wash my fives"; and the game may originally have been played between two teams each of five players.
fixtures: a pocket sized compendium carried by almost every Etonian, which includes the *half's* sports events.
The Fourth: the everyday name for the *Fourth of June*.
The Fourth of June: Eton's sports day celebrating George III's birthday. It is also called *The Glorious Fourth*, but not by Etonians.
furking: a foul in the *field game*.

georgic: a punishment. The boy has to copy out Latin verse from Virgil's poem on farming called the *'Georgics'*, which he wrote in 30 B.C.
gig: a wide boat used by *dry bobs* because it is very difficult to capsize.
goal: a score in the *field game* worth three points.

half: term. The word originates from the days when the school year was divided into two halves. To describe half-term, Etonians have resisted the temptation to coin the word 'half-half'. Instead they call it *long leave* (Charterhouse's word for term is 'quarter').
half change: the same as *school dress* except that instead of the tail coat and waistcoat, you wear a sports jacket.
half holiday: the days of week (Tuesday, Thursday and Saturday) when there are *divs* before but not after *boy's dinner*.
head man: the *head master*.
head master: Eton's headmaster is spelt as two words. But the boys usually referred to him as the *head man*.
head master's assembly: an occasion every few weeks when *Upper School* assembles to hear the *head man*.
Hencoop: the area in *Lower Chapel* reserved for *new boys*.
hexameter: a line of Latin verse with six metres.
holy poker: College Chapel's verger, who leads important guests with his verge (wand) held high above his head.
house: a group of about fifty boys who live together in the same house. The word also refers to the house itself.
housemaster: the master in charge of each *house*.

irregulars: irregular verbs, either Latin or French.

Jordan: a tributary of the Thames, which meanders along the edge of Mesopotamia, one of Eton's playing fields.
Judy's Passage: a narrow walled pathway leading from the centre of Eton to a group of boy's *houses*.

K.S.: abbreviation for *King's Scholar*.
Keeper of the College Wall: captain of the *College Wall*.
Keeper of the Field: captain of the *Field*, Eton's top *field game* team.

Keeper of the Oppidan Wall: captain of the *Oppidan Wall*.
King's Scholar: tug.
kneeler football: a game played in Chapel. The Chapel kneelers are used instead of a ball. The rules are closer to those of the *wall game* than the *field game*, the pew representing the *wall*.
kneeling on the ball: a foul in the *field game*.
knife boards: the rows of pews on each side of the aisle in *College Chapel*, which are barely wide enough to sit on.

Latin construe: translation from a Latin text.
leaver: 1 a leaving boy.
　　　2 a photograph of an Etonian which he gives to his friends when he leaves Eton. He usually adds a short farewell message alongside.
library: 1 the self-elective governing body of each *house*, made up of Etonians in their last year.
　　　2 the room belonging to members of *library*, where they have a television set and refrigerator.
library table: washing the *library's* dishes as a punishment.
lights out: the time when you have to be in bed with your lights out. In your first *half*, it is at 9.00pm. Thereafter, it is at 9.30pm until you are in *C-block*, when it is at 10.00pm.
lock-up: the time when you have to be in your *house*. The doors are actually locked.
Lower Chapel: the chapel used by Etonians in *E* and *F-blocks*, which was built to take the overflow from *College Chapel*. The area in *Lower Chapel* reserved for *new boys* is called the *Hencoop*.
lower man: the *lower master*.
lower master: the *beak* in charge of *Lower School* (boys in *E* and *F-blocks*). He is called the *lower man* by the boys.
Lower School: the subdivision of the school consisting of boys in *E* and *F-blocks*.

Ma: short for *Major*, the elder of two brothers.
Mi: short for *Minor*, the younger of two brothers.
marking out: the system by which Etonians who shirk Chapel are caught.
matron-in-college: the *dame* of *College*.
modern tutor: the *beak* who succeeds your *classical tutor* as your academic supervisor once you are sixteen. You can select him yourself.
monarch: a boat in the *Procession of Boats* with ten oars and ten oarsmen.
moss picking: scraping moss from the stones of School Yard as a punishment.
move before: a foul in the *field game*.

new boy: an Etonian in his first *half*.

O.E.: abbreviation for Old Etonian.
O.S.: abbreviation for *Oppidan Scholar*.
on the bill: if you are *on the head master's bill* or *lower master's bill*, you have to appear before one of these figures.
oppidan: an Etonian who is not a *tug*. The word derives from the Latin *oppidum* meaning town. Originally, the *tugs* (or scholars) lived in the college buildings at the expense of the school and the others lived in boarding houses in the town.
Oppidan Scholar: an honorary scholar who does not live in *College* or get free education.
Oppidan wall: a *wall game* team made up of the strongest *oppidans*.
order card: a report on your academic performance each month. The classical *order card* is issued fortnightly.

passing: a foul in the *field game*.
pentameter: a line of Latin verse with five metres.

Peter Fleming Owl: a bronze owl, awarded for the best contribution to the *Chronicle* each *half*. In memory of Peter Fleming O.E.

playing on the ground: a foul in the *field game*.

pop: short for popular, it is the Etonian's everyday name for the *Eton Society*, the self-elective club of Eton.

pop material: an Etonian thought by his contemporaries to have a chance of getting into *pop*.

pop patrol: a tour by members of *pop* of the local pubs, in search of out-of-bounds and rule-breaking Etonians.

popper: a member of *pop*.

Pop Wall: a wall located in Long Walk, upon which only members of *pop* are allowed to sit.

post: the least coveted position in the *field game*.

praepostor: from the Latin *praepositor* meaning overseer. An ambassador of the *head man* who summons Etonians for questioning or punishment.

President of Pop: The *President of Pop* is elected by the other members of *pop*. He meet regularly with the *head man* to discuss *pop's* responsibilities.

Procession of Boats: the boating event of the *Fourth of June*.

provost: elected by the *fellows*, he is the chairman of Eton's governing body.

Rafts: the area around the boathouses.

The Ramblers: a cricket team made up of Old Etonians.

ram: 1 a human battering ram used in the *field game* to convert a *rouge* to a *goal* (or *rammed rouge*.) There are stories of O.E.s forming *rams* at Oxford drinks parties.
  2 *ram* is also used to describe the column of important guests, staff and boys who march into *College Chapel* led by the *holy poker*.

rammed rouge: a *goal* scored by successfully *ramming* a *rouge*.

rigger: the type of sculling boat used by first year *wet bobs*.

rip: a bad piece of work is ripped by the *beak*. It then has to be shown to the boy's *housemaster* and *classical* or *modern tutor*. Some of the older beaks still call them *tear overs*.

rouge: a touchdown in the *field game* worth two points.

Rowlands: the tuck shop.

run: if a *beak* is more than fifteen minutes late for a *div*, the boys are entitled to run from the school room.

rusticate: to expel from Eton on a temporary basis, usually for the remainder of the *half*.

school dress: Eton's black and white uniform, which includes a tail coat, waistcoat, pin striped trousers, starched collar and white tie.

sent up for good: given to a boy for an exceptionally good piece of work, which is shown to the *head man* and his *tutors*.

sermon cricket: more of a gambling game than a cricket game. It is based on the number of "Ummms" and "Ahhhs" in a sermon. Almost extinct.

show up: a good piece of work is marked "Show up" by the *beak*. The boy can show it to his *tutors*.

side post the name of each player in the *field game* who supports the *post*.

sixth form select: a group of the twenty leading scholars in the sixth form chosen on purely academic grounds according to their *trials* performance over the years. Their number is usually made up of ten K.S. and ten O.S., including the *Captain of the School* and the *Captain of the Oppidans*.

slab: the long sideboard in each *house* where Etonians congregate.

slack bob: technically a boy in the Summer *half*, who is neither a *wet bob* nor a *dry bob*. It also describes someone who avoids playing sports at any time of the year.

Slough Comprehensive: in a spirit of questionable modesty, Etonians sometimes answer the question, "Where do you go to school?" with "*Slough Comprehensive*".

sneaking: a foul in the *field game*.

sock: to buy food for another Etonian. The word originates from the sockads (meaning sellers of food) who used to congregate in the centre of Eton during the nineteenth century.

Speeches: an occasion on the *Fourth of June* when *Sixth Form Select* display their oratory skills by reciting well-known passages.

standard change: a jacket and tie. You cannot wear jeans.

St. Andrew's Day: the Saturday closest to November 30th.

steeplechase: the annual cross country run.

stick-ups: white bow tie and wing collar. Worn by Etonians who have succeeded, in one of a variety of different ways.

swot: an Etonian who studies intensively.

swotting: studying intensively.

tails: tail coat.

taking leave: an appointment with the *head man* at the end of your Eton career.

Tap: the school's pub. In 1954 *Tap* became a club to avoid the licensing restrictions of a pub.

Tap bore: an Etonian who is a regular at *Tap*.

tardy book: a punishment for being late, which dates from the early nineteenth century.

trials: school exams at the end of most *halves*.

tug: the Etonian's name for the scholar of Eton. Also called *King's Scholar* and *Colleger*. Some think that the word *tug* derives from the Latin *togati* meaning gowned. Others say that the *tugs* got their name by the *oppidans* always tugging at their gowns.

tutors: used in the plural, it refers to a boy's *housemaster* and *classical tutor* or *modern tutor*.

Upper School: the subdivision of the school consisting of boys over sixteen.

vice provost: the *provost's* deputy, usually a former *housemaster*.

Wall: the long and high wall running along the side of College Field, after which the *wall game* was named.

wall game: a ball game unique to Eton, which is played against the *Wall*.

wet: technically it means pathetic, but Etonians also use the word as a general insult.

wet bob: a rower.

white ticket: a punishment given for lack of academic succcess or effort.

white triangle: a *white triangle* exists when your white shirt can be seen under the 'V' of your waistcoat.